Why Can't I

Land

A

Job?

The Rigmarole of The Hiring System

Dr. Chalette Renee Griffin, SHRM-CP

www.foresight-for-the-new-age-recruiter.com
www.linkedin.com/in/drgriffincr0924

DEDICATION

To all the men and women who want
and need to work

CONTENTS

ACKNOWLEDGMENTS

I want to thank my HR colleagues who shared their experiences being on the other side of the hiring system.

IS THIS BOOK FOR ME?

This book is for anyone who is looking for work. The circumstances that placed you or the person you care about in the position of landing a job does not define you or your loved one. Earning a paycheck starts with creating an intervention in the method in which you are looking for a job. So, I will not insult your intelligence by including unemployment figures and statistics in this book, since these numbers will not help you in landing a job.

Applicants, Candidates, and Job Seekers

Before we get started, I need to explain two terms that will be referenced throughout this book, 'applicant' and 'candidate'[1]. Although some people use these terms interchangeably, the two words have different meanings within the selection and hiring system. The term 'applicant' means a person who submitted a resume and/or employment application to a position. In other words, applicants officially show interest in a job by providing the appropriate documentation as requested by the employer.

On the other hand, when a recruiter contacts an applicant for an interview, the applicant becomes a 'candidate' for the job. Since using the terms 'applicant' and 'candidate' can confuse the reader, the word 'job seekers' will be used to mean applicants and/or candidates throughout this book.

Semantics of the Hiring System Exposed

When job seekers invest in the time to understand the complexities of the hiring system, they can leverage it to their advantage in landing a job. Why? Because there are hidden hiring practices and assumptions that harm job seekers in landing a job. It is my professional view the lack of exposure to how the hiring system operates has hurt job seekers professionally and personally.

Once job seekers understand the big picture of how hiring works within HR, they will be exposed to alternative methods to increase their chances of landing a job.

No Quick Solutions

However, this book is not for people who are unwilling or reluctant to explore alternative methods to use the current hiring system better to land a job. The alternative job-seeking methods will require some latitude of creativity and courage by job seekers to step outside their comfort zone. This book is not for job seekers who are looking for a quick solution to landing a job or 'secrets' to landing one. There are already enough obscurities within the hiring system, which is hindering job seekers from finding work. I do not want to add any more underlying assumptions about a hiring system already built on an air of exclusivity.

No 'Vent Fest' Here

This book is not a 'vent fest' against human resources
and recruiting professionals since my closest friends
and colleagues serve in the profession. I merely
disagree with the method in which my HR colleagues
select and hire people for jobs. Why? Because the
hiring system is elusive and misleading to job seekers.
Furthermore, I believe the elusiveness of the hiring
system is contributing to the vast amount of eager and
hard-working people unable to land a job. There are so
many people who want to work, but unable to land a
job. I do not believe job seekers are solely to blame for
this - something else is going on here. It is my
professional view the hiring system is obstructing
people's opportunity in being visible to recruiters and
hiring managers.

To get a feel for the book, here is a brief synopsis of
each chapter:

INTRODUCTION: Explains why recruiters and HR
professionals use the term 'rejected' to describe job
seekers who have not met their hiring expectations as
well as the insignificance of it.

CHAPTER 1: Describes six reasons why it is so
difficult to land a job.

CHAPTER 2: Explains HR's purpose and relevance
in the selection and hiring procedures.

CHAPTER 3: Describes how job seekers information is assessed and evaluated to determine who is hired. This chapter also exposes uncontrollable factors and events within the hiring system which negatively impacts job seekers.

CHAPTER 4: Explains why the inability to land a job is not job seeker's fault. Also, the chapter discusses the irrational viewpoint of critics who believe job seekers are solely to blame for their unsuccessful job search.

CHAPTER 5: Discusses hidden and uncontrollable factors outside of ATS, data management technique, bias and discrimination which interferes with the visibility of job seekers landing a job.

CHAPTER 6: Encourages job seekers to channel their emotions into productive actions which lead to landing a job, rather than lashing out against human resources professionals.

CHAPTER 7: Explores four practical and utilized methods for job seekers to gain visibility in the hiring system and the importance of leaving their comfort zone in how they found employment in the past. The chapter also provides explanations to why it is vital to 'go around' HR in the hiring system.

CHAPTER 8: Provides an explanation to why recruiters and HR professionals are against job seekers finding alternative solutions to landing a job. Also, the chapter discusses why HR professionals need job seekers to continue to follow the status quo of hiring.

CHAPTER 9 & 10: Shares a letter a job seeker sent to a recruiter to explain the problems within the hiring system. The job seeker includes 24 reasons why the hiring system is ineffective to job seekers.

CHAPTER 11: Describes why job seekers must focus on their mental health and explore ways to help decrease job search depression.

CHAPTER 12: Encourages job seekers to possess the strength and grit to preserve and improve their family's quality of life by landing a job. Also, the chapter reiterates the importance of job seekers to land a job on their terms, and not HR's.

INTRODUCTION:
I'M NOT A 'REJECT'!

So, who is a rejected job seeker? A rejected job seeker is someone who continually applies to positions of employment for an extended time and is unable to land a job. Rejected job seekers are people who are degreed, non-degreed, experienced as well as less experienced individuals who comes from various sectors, industries, and social and economic backgrounds. Although, some readers may find the term 'rejected' offensive, HR and the hiring manager do not care how they define you, as a job seeker, in the hiring system – especially for those who they deem as 'unqualified' based on their hiring system. Besides, HR professionals use the term to describe you a job seeker, who did not meet their expectations within the hiring system.

The internet is loaded with articles, blogs, and websites which discuss why recruiters reject job seekers. All you need to do is just type 'why job candidates or applicants are rejected' in the Google search engine to receive millions of returns on the subject. Tables 1 and 2 list a few reasons why recruiters will bypass applicants and candidates. Please note the tables below do not represent every reason, but some of the most popular ones. However, as I said at the beginning of this book, how HR describes you in the hiring system, does not define you as a human being. Do not let those automated generic rejection letters from the applicant tracking system validate your worth.

Do not let anyone or anything tell you that you are not employable, not even HR. Let's be clear that you are in the fight of your life. Why? Because you and your family's quality of life is at stake. Now is not the time to be passive or scared. So, put on your thick armor of perseverance, resilience, and grit – because you will need all of these attributes to land a job.

Table 1: Reasons Applicants Are Rejected

Resume loaded with spelling typos and grammatical errors	Exaggerated experience and accomplishments	Not enough experience
Too much experience	Resume lack keywords	Unexplained employment gaps
Lack of computer and technical skills	Resume too long	Outdated skills and experience
Live too far	Skills mismatch	Not enough education
Too much education	Fancy fonts and invalid characters in resume	Lack of accomplishments and relevant performance
Unattractive resume format	Poor academic performance	Lack of relevant experience

The main problem which is contributing to the cycle of being unemployed is job seekers inability to successfully navigate the hiring system due to no fault of their own. Why? Because the method in which job seekers are taught how to land a job no longer works. The past success of responding to a job vacancy and waiting for HR to contact job seekers about the next steps no longer holds in the 21st century. As a result of applicant tracking software, HR will not even get the opportunity to read every resume, which meets the qualifications in the job.

Table 2: Reasons Candidates Are Rejected

Poor interview skills	Lack of self confidence	Too confident
Overly aggressive personality	Not assertive enough	Clueless about the company
Appearance	Too nervous	Unable to articulate skills needed for the job
Habitual name dropping	Just looking for a paycheck	Low energy (code word for too old)
No enthusiasm or excitement for role	More interested in salary than essential functions	Didn't function well under pressure
Arrived late for the interview	Poor body language/lack of eye contact	Unpolished/lack professionalism

Even when candidates take the 'dos and don'ts' advice of recruiters and hiring managers as noted in Tables 1 and 2, the instructions are not enough to advance in the hiring system. In essence, job seekers, for the most part, are following the advice of recruiters, hiring managers, career coaches, and hiring experts, and still, find themselves unemployed. As a result of this disparity, job seekers must realize the hiring process is a 'system'.

Process vs. System

The term 'process' is loosely defined as activities, steps, or actions used to preserve something to achieve a result. A process provides consistency to achieve a desired outcome[2]. However, for a process to ensure consistency, the activities within it must follow some predictable form and have transparency. For people to participate in a process, they must know all of the activities, steps and actions, in a process to govern within it.

Based on the above explanation, the term 'hiring process' does not make sense, since job seekers assume, they know all of the activities, steps, and actions in the hiring process. Also, the hiring process is not transparent, and the activities within the hiring process do not follow a predictable or logical path. Why? Because recruiters and hiring managers often make changes to the activities, steps, and actions within the hiring process to how they see fit, without informing job seekers of the changes. For example, recruiters and hiring managers tell applicants that they will be contacted if their qualifications and background meet their needs. On the other hand, the recruiters and hiring managers contradict themselves by telling applicants that they may not be contacted although they have met the qualifications in the job posting.

The contradiction suggests there are other factors and criteria in the hiring process that are unexposed to job seekers. In other words, there are other steps, actions, methods, and components in the hiring process, which are unbeknownst to job seekers, which leads to unpredictability. Applicants have no clue when or if a recruiter will ever reach out to them. A process is required to offer consistency and transparency. If hiring is defined as a process, then applicants would know if a recruiter will contact them. If applicants have no idea if a recruiter will ever reach out to them, then how is hiring a 'process'? Since the hiring process is unpredictable and lacks transparency for applicants and candidates, hiring is not a process, but a system.

What is a System?

A system is a collective of parts which interact with each other to function as a whole[3]. A system can be comprised of people, things, places, and yes, processes working as one unit.[4] In essence, a system is comprised of anything and anyone working as a collective. Also, parts in a system can be known or unknown. In other words, there are components in the hiring system which are unidentified in hiring and ultimately hurt job seekers. The unidentified parts in a system are people, things, processes, and events. Sometimes, no one has control over the unknown parts due to their unpredictable nature of how and when they influence a direction or flow in a collective. Since we identified that a process is required to offer consistency, in which in hiring, it does not. The definition of a system aligns to what happens in hiring because the inability to identify all of the people, trends, conditions, processes, events, and behaviors, which influence hiring, are unpredictable. So, hiring is not a process, but a system, due to the inability to precisely know which factors are impacting and influencing how people are selected and hired.

A hiring system is unbalanced, undependable, and complex. Why? Because the system draws its strength from a lack of universal standards and rules which allows recruiters and hiring managers to use the randomness of the system to their advantage. Biased and unpredictable behaviors of human beings and unforgiving software applications make the hiring system impossible to master as a job seeker to land a job. There is just too many competing known and unknown factors which are beyond the control of job seekers to make the hiring system balanced and fair to them.

So, what does the hiring system looks like?

The hiring system is a 3-point framework that people are told and taught to follow to get hired for a job as noted in Figure 1. However, there are several problems with the hiring system which are continuing to stifle job seekers in landing a job:

- The hiring system is more technical with less human contact. Applicant tracking software is a big reason why applicants are unable to advance in the hiring system[5]. Some qualified resumes do not see the light of day because the software does not select them.

Figure 1: Hiring System

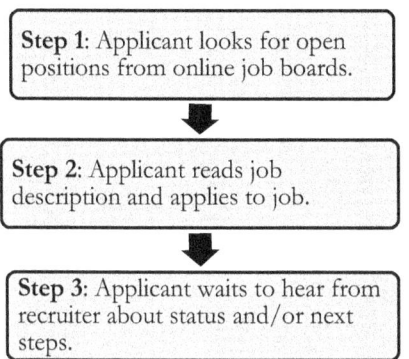

Source: Griffin, C.R. (June 3, 2019). Recruiter's transition to a future-focused method of hiring from 2030 and beyond. *Amazon.com*.

- The hiring system is not set up to review every applicant's resume to a position. On average corporate job openings receive 250 resumes[6]. Even the resumes which meet the qualifications may not receive the attention of the recruiter nor the hiring manager. From 250 applicants, only 4-6 candidates will receive an interview and one of the interviewed candidates will get the job[7]. Here's another way to explain the above statistic. For every open position, a job seeker applied on an online job board, an estimate of 249 people has also applied to the same job. The hiring system is not designed to screen every applicant who applies to an online job.

DON'T GET COMFORTABLE WITH BEING 'REJECTED'

There have been many articles written about the importance of job seekers to get comfortable with receiving rejection letters and not to take them personally. Ignoring the pesky messages are easier said than done. The average time for people to land a job is five months. Job seekers who have been out of work longer than six months must consider evaluating the method they are utilizing to land a job. If job seekers are solely responding to job ads and waiting for HR to contact them, then this is not an effective strategy. This type of job hunting will only keep the rejection letters coming.

Unfortunately, rejection letters serve as psychological reminders of disappointments and let downs that can wreak havoc on your confidence. Receiving a bunch of these rejection letters is something job seekers should not 'get used to' and normalize as part of the job search.

The good news is there are ways to leverage the hiring system to gain some power and control over how recruiters treat you as an applicant and candidate. The goal for job seekers is to become visible to recruiters and hiring managers in the hiring system. However, for job seekers to become visible in the hiring system, they must first understand the authentic way the hiring system operates.

1 WHY IS IT SO HARD TO LAND A JOB THESE DAYS?

There are 6 reasons why it is so difficult to land a job in the 21st century.

1. **Job seekers own bias about the hiring system.** Job seekers expectations of what the hiring system is and isn't are holding them back from landing a job. There is a disconnect between what job seekers think of how the hiring system works and the underlying assumptions of how the hiring system works in reality.

   The false notion of how hiring works is not job seekers fault, since they are doing what they were taught in how to land a job. The hiring system is so far-fetched than what job seekers imagined in their heads. Based on my HR professional experience, job seekers make the following assumptions about recruiters, hiring managers, and the hiring system:

   - **The method in which employers assess job seekers skillsets is fair and reliable**. Job seekers blindly trust the method in which employers assess their skillsets. Why? Since they are considered the experts, job seekers assume the employer has their best interest in determining their fit in the job.

- **The hiring system always ends with the best of the best person hired for the job.** Many job seekers assume that if they didn't get the job, they were not qualified to perform in the role. Don't you dare believe that!

- **The hiring system is logical and follows a pattern, which is a big assumption by many job seekers.** Think about it, if the hiring system is logical, then why applicants are not told by recruiters when they will reach out to them to discuss the status of their candidacy for a job? There is absolutely nothing logical about applicants having to wonder if they will ever hear back from a recruiter.

- **Job seekers who follow all of the steps in the hiring system will always get hired.** Job seekers have been taught to believe if they follow all of the rules and advice by recruiters, hiring managers, career advisors and hiring experts, concerning how to get hired, they will land a job.

- **Job seekers who meet all of the qualifications in the job will get hired.** There are many times applicants know they should have heard from a recruiter, since they have performed the same duties in their current position, or similar duties in a previous role. For some reason, they never hear from a recruiter. Even job seekers who possess the same job title as in the open vacancy, do not receive a call from a recruiter.

- **Candidates who answer all of the interview questions flawlessly will get hired.** There is this notion that if candidates answer every question flawlessly, they will advance in the hiring system and land the job. Job seekers learn that employers measure their qualifications based on how well they answer the behavioral interview questions. Based on how candidates answer their questions will determine whether they advance to the next hiring phase. Experts noted that rating candidates responses to their questions is not a reliable method to learn about a candidate's abilities to perform in a job[8]. Why? Because job seekers can meet the qualifications for the job and perform horribly answering the behavioral interview questions.

For example, if candidates are unable to articulate where they see themselves in five years, does it mean that they are unable to manage projects or create pivot tables in Excel? Or if candidates answer the behavioral interview questions flawlessly, does it mean that they will perform successfully in the role? There is no connection between answering the behavioral interview questions perfectly and successfully performing the essential functions of the job[9]. Nor is there a correlation between answering the questions flawlessly and getting hired.

- **Job seekers who experience a 'connection' with a recruiter and hiring manager will get hired.** This assumption is a popular one among applicants and candidates. Job seekers assume having a conversation about last night episode of 'The Masked Singer' or showing pictures of their dog waterskiing from their mobile device will help them get hired. The recruiter and hiring manager are being nice to you. That's it.

- **Recruiters and hiring managers want to get to know job seekers personally.** Many job seekers believe that recruiters and hiring managers want to know their hobbies or obligations outside of the responsibilities of the job. They want to get to know job seekers professionally, not personally.

- **The only way to land a job is through human resources.** Job seekers assume that for every open position, they must go through human resources, which is false. However, if the job you are seeking is an HR position, then yes, you are in the right department. For job seekers who are applying to non- HR jobs, the human resources department should not be your only connection and resource for the job.

When job seekers remove their assumptions about what the hiring system should and should not do, they can begin to build an authentic strategy in how to become visible to recruiters and hiring managers.

2. Increased Competition Among Candidates

Long-term unemployed people are not the only job seekers looking for work. There is increased competition with recent high school and college graduates, people who are re-entering the workforce and career changers. Even employees are among the competitors for internal positions posted to external job boards. The labor pool is filled with all types of people with various backgrounds seeking employment.

3. Technology

Many employers transitioned to an online hiring application process. Job seekers who do not have access to the internet will not have the ability to apply to jobs online. The preferred method to apply for a job is online by many employers. It is no wonder that 60 percent of job seekers are forced to find work using online job boards[10].

4. HR Doesn't Communicate To Job Seekers

Since there are so many job seekers applying to jobs, it is impossible for recruiters to personally talk to every single one of them about their application status. Think about it. If a recruiter had to speak to 250 applicants per day, he or she would not be able to perform other duties.

To be candid, recruiters do not want to talk to applicants anyway. Why? Because recruiters do not want to say something which can be interpreted by job seekers as discriminatory. On the job posting, recruiters even tell job seekers not to contact them nor the HR department about the position or application status. I'm sure you have seen the 'no phone calls please' on the job ads.

Although the word 'human' is in human resources, it is clear that the inability for job seekers to communicate with recruiters makes it difficult for them to get feedback about how they stack up to their competitors for the job.

5. Government Compliance and Reporting

Before government compliance, most corporations were able to hire who they wanted, even if applicants did not necessarily meet the qualifications for the job. As a result of discriminatory hiring practices, many companies have to report to the government who they hired under the Affirmative Action Plan. Companies who meet the criteria of being federal contractors or subcontractors who have fifty or more employees AND having a contract of $50,000 or more are subject to participate in the Affirmative Action Program under the U.S. Department of Labor Office of Federal Contract Compliance[11],[12].

The Plan show the race and gender of the candidate hired for a respective position. This information is captured when applicants complete the EEO-1(Equal Employment Opportunity) Voluntary Self-Identification Forms at the end of the employment application. The Plan also details where the employer posted the open position. The Government Compliance and Reporting have prohibited employers from hiring people without a business justification for the individual to serve in the role. To satisfy goals within the Affirmative Action Plan[13], some candidates will not be selected for the position, even though they were qualified.

6. Bias and Discrimination Within the Hiring System

Unfortunately, many job seekers are unable to land a job due to bias and discrimination in the hiring system. Although this practice is illegal, recruiters and hiring managers have discriminated against job seekers for various reasons. The most prevalent bias and discrimination in hiring is age discrimination. For job seekers 40 years of age and older, it is more difficult for them to land jobs. Sometimes information contained in resumes can reveal an applicant's age, such as:

- When applicants include dates when they graduated from high school or college.
- When applicants include 15 years of experience and more in their resume.

- When applicants include outdated job titles and industry terms in their resume.
- When applicants include outdated experience and computer/technical skills.
- When applicants do not include social media handles via LinkedIn or personal website on their resume.
- When applicants include discharge dates from military service.

It is unfortunate that job seekers over 40 have been discriminated against from recruiters and hiring managers. However, the idea that the U.S workforce can only comprise of people under 40 is unrealistic. Since half of the U.S. population is over 38 years old[14], recruiters and hiring managers will need to hire older workers to fill jobs. Now that you have a general understanding of the various factors which are sabotaging your opportunity to land a job, let's explore HR's role in your job search.

2 WHY IS HR IN THE HIRING BUSINESS?

There are plenty of articles and blogs which discuss whether HR should continue to serve in the business of finding and selecting talent or transition the responsibility to hiring managers. However, HR is still needed in the transaction of finding and selecting people for three reasons:

1. The System is Free From Discrimination

This section contradicts the end of Chapter 1 about bias and discrimination in the selection and hiring system by recruiters and hiring managers. However, HR's role is to ensure that people are hired fairly based on the Equal Employment Opportunity Policy (EEO) policy. What EEO policy? The disclaimer at the bottom of the job description, careers websites and employment applications. The disclaimer may look similar to this below:

"All qualified applicants will receive consideration for employment without regard to race, color, religion, sex, sexual orientation, age, gender, identity, national origin or protected veteran status and will not be discriminated against on the basis of disability"

Equal Opportunity/Disability/Veteran Employer

HR's role is to make sure that all who are involved in the selection and hiring of talent follow the EEO

Policy to avoid potential liability from alleged discriminatory hiring practices. Although ensuring fair hiring practices is still an area HR struggles with as a profession, they are responsible for upholding the EEO policy. HR professionals are also responsible for training and enforcing hiring managers to follow the federal mandate.

Let's be clear that not all recruiters and hiring managers are utilizing discriminatory practices. There are people in HR who are trying to do the legal and proper way of hiring people. On the other hand, it is essential to note that recruiters and hiring managers who indeed discriminate against job seekers are some reasons why they are unable to land a job.

2. Find the Most Qualified Person

Another reason HR is in the hiring business is to find qualified people to serve in the organization. Applicants and candidates must be properly vetted to ensure they bring the necessary education, skills, and knowledge to perform in the jobs. HR is needed to help hiring managers find people to fill roles. Hiring managers are the ones who actually make the decision to who is hired in their respective team or department, not HR. Unless, the position is in HR, of course.

3. Meet the Minimum Qualifications

Lastly, HR is in the hiring business to make sure that applicants meet the qualifications in the job. Applicants who do not meet the minimum requirements to perform in the role do not advance to the next hiring phase.

What is ironic about HR's role is that all applicants who meet the qualifications in the job still do not advance to the next hiring phase. Many applicants will not have the opportunity for HR to review their resumes, as a result of the hiring system not designed to review all resumes submitted for the position. HR's role and their progress in being 'shepherds of hiring,' is questionable based on the current discrimination and bias infecting the hiring system. Job seekers need to understand HR's place in hiring. However, there are other factors that job seekers need to know about the hiring system to help them land a job.

3 WHAT I NEED TO KNOW ABOUT THE HIRING SYSTEM?

Once job seekers complete the on-line job application process and hit the submit button to solidify their candidacy for the position, what happens to all that information? Where does it go?

Welcome to the World of Applicant Tracking Systems

Applicant tracking systems (ATS) help companies automate the way they manage their entire recruiting process, from receiving applications to hiring employees[15]. ATS is simply a database where applicants' contact information, education credentials, experience, and other job-related documents are stored. When applicants apply for a job online, their information is stored in a database where the system rate their qualifications based on keywords before a recruiter lay eyes on the material (Figure 2).

ATS enables recruiters to move applicants and candidates through the selection and hiring cycle through generating and sending automated emails to confirm receipt of employment application, schedule interviews, send offer and rejection letters and new hire orientation information[16]. Many recruiters would argue that applicant tracking systems have improved their hiring process since they can easily track and manage candidates in one organized database[17]. Once ATS scan and rate applicants' resumes based on keywords, recruiters can begin to narrow the applicant pool.

How Does Recruiters Narrow The Applicant Pool?

As mentioned in the last section, ATS selects resumes which have keywords from the job description, or other specific criteria recruiters may input as a search criterion such as bachelor's degree, business administration, salary or location to narrow the pool.

Random Criterion

For example, recruiters are permitted to use some random criteria which is not discriminatory to continue to narrow the applicant pool. Organizations under the Affirmative Action Plan will need to document the specific criteria used to narrow down the applicant pool to ensure it is free from discrimination and bias[18].

Let's say that a job vacancy for an executive assistant position received 250 applicants. From the 250 applicants, ATS selected 100 applicants resumes which included keywords related to the position. So, how does the recruiter narrow 100 applicants to a manageable pool to begin the interview process? Through data management technique.

Figure 2: Screen Shot of Applicant Tracking System

C 🔒 https://www.talentlists.com/pages/screenshots   ☆

Hello Technologies   Home | Job openings | Talents | Company ▾ | Account ▾ | Help

Candidates for DIRECTOR - HR BUSINESS PARTNERS

| First name | Last name | Email | Status | **Search** |

First Name	Last Name	Gender	Age	Email	Status	Actions
Lauriane	Collier	Male	21	abdiel_flatley@trompjenkins.net	initial	View / Remove
Brain	MacGyver	Male	40	alfonso@wolf.name	initial	View / Remove
Reta	Hyatt	Male	43	anne.waters@smitham.com	waiting_for_interview	View / Remove
Gillian	Moore	Female	37	astrid@lynch.com	initial	View / Remove
Emmett	Jerde	Male	43	barry@herzog.com	pending	View / Remove
Elvis	Maggio	Male	44	bertram@fritsch.info	initial	View / Remove
Wilbert	Satterfield	Male	38	cara@tillman.name	waiting_for_interview	View / Remove
Webster	Champlin	Male	32	domenica.lind@effertz.name	waiting_for_interview	View / Remove
Gus	Hamill	Female	26	drake@oreilly.name	initial	View / Remove
Dewayne	Tremblay	Female	33	edwin@lindgren.com	initial	View / Remove
Linwood	Paucek	Female	38	elisa@quigley.com	initial	View / Remove
Isai	Moore	Female	33	enoch_upton@olsonbatz.net	initial	View / Remove
Elinore	Wilkinson	Female	27	estelle@mclaughlin.net	waiting_for_interview	View / Remove
		Male	34	freddie_block@teschmayert.name	initial	View / Remove

www.talentlists.com/pages/screenshots#carousel-casts

Source: www.talentlists.com/pages/screenshots

However, if the pool is still significant, then recruiters must use more inclusive criteria which will 'knock out' a higher number of applicants to narrow the pool.

Data Management Technique

Data management technique enables recruiters to use several expressions to narrow the pool. As long as the criteria do not create "any disparate impact based on race, gender, or ethnicity in the expressions of interest considered"[19]. So, back to our scenario of a recruiter having to narrow down 100 applicants. Let's say that the recruiter needs to narrow the pool to 20 percent of 100 in the applicant pool, which is 20 qualified applicants. For the recruiter to narrow the pool to the first 20 qualified applicants, a recruiter may decide to review applicants who applied within a specific period, Monday to Wednesday, for example.

At this point, the recruiter will review the resumes of those applicants who applied between Monday and Wednesday to get 20 qualified applicants. However, the recruiter may reach the first 20 qualified applicants from those who applied to the position on Monday and therefore, do not need to review applicants who applied on Tuesday or Wednesday. In other cases, the recruiter may need to consider applicants beyond Wednesday since the applicants who applied between Monday to Wednesday were unqualified. There are many techniques the recruiter utilizes to narrow down the pool. Some recruiters may review every other applicant within a specific period as well. As I stated before, the recruiter is permitted to use a random technique as long as it does not consider race, gender, or ethnicity as part of the criteria.

How Is This Relevant to Me Looking for Work?

So, let's continue to use the executive assistant position to further explain how the applicant tracking system and data management technique impacts applicants in the selection process. If an applicant applied to the job and received an automated rejection letter, below are some of the reasons why. Some reasons may not necessarily have anything to do with applicants lack of preparation nor qualifications:

- **The resume was not selected based on ATS, although the applicant met the minimum qualifications of the job.** For example, a lack of keywords, formatting issues such as bullets and tables, or the layout of the resume itself can disrupt the sensitive nature of ATS. As a result, some resumes are invisible to recruiters since some ATS are more sensitive than others.

A job seeker's resume is successful from the applicant tracking system from Company A. While the same resume may reach the ATS black hole from Company B. It is a game of hit and miss with ATS.

- **The resume was not selected because the applicant applied on a day outside of the recruiter's review criteria.** Applicants who applied to the executive assistant position on Thursday and the remainder of the week were not contenders for the job. Although they may have met the minimum qualifications, the applicants and recruiter will never know for sure. The method baffles some applicants who believe if they apply for a position within the time noted on the job description, they will be considered for the job. For example, the executive assistant position was posted for five days, from Monday the 1st to Friday the 5th. Applicants who applied for the position between the specified period may not be selected to be reviewed based on recruiters utilizing data management technique to narrow the pool. In this case, the recruiter only reviewed applicants who applied on Monday, the 1st to Wednesday, the 3rd, although applicants were instructed to apply for the job from Monday, the 1st to Friday, the 5th.

- **The resume was not selected because the recruiter received enough qualified applicants.** Let's say that an applicant was the 21st person to apply for the executive assistant position on Monday. In this case, the applicant applied for the job outside of the recruiter's review criteria of the first 20 qualified applicants.

- **The resume was not selected because the recruiter read it and deemed the applicant unqualified for the job**. In this case, the applicant's resume made it past ATS but did not qualify for further consideration.

All the Steps in The Hiring System Are Not Disclosed to Applicants

Of course, the random criteria recruiters utilize to narrow the applicant pool is not disclosed to applicants and candidates. The type of data management technique recruiters select determines whether an applicant advances in the next hiring phase or receives an automated rejection letter. As noted, there are plenty of reasons why applicants are not visible to recruiters. Applicants do not know which data management technique a recruiter will utilize to narrow the pool. Nor which ATS is more suited to the applicants' resume format for it to become visible to a recruiter. Job seekers do not have control over how ATS impacts them, even though a handful of applicants will benefit from it.

At this point, maybe you think the whole hiring system sucks and you are right. ATS and data management technique are some components which are holding job seekers from landing a job. Many job seekers believe they were rejected because they were not the most qualified person for the job. And unfortunately, HR wants job seekers to think that as well.

They want you to believe there are preparational aspects of the job search that job seekers are not doing to make themselves successful in landing a job. Job seekers do not have a clue to whether ATS will accept their resume format or which data management technique recruiters will utilize to narrow the applicant pool, or other internal factors unknown and out of their control.

So, how can applicants be blamed for parts of the hiring system unknown to them? Is it applicants fault they can't land a job?

4 IS IT MY FAULT I CAN'T LAND A JOB?

Job seekers have followed the advice of professionals by investing time and money in resume preparation, mock interview participation, and appropriate dress for success interview instructions. In addition, job seekers study the same old behavioral interview questions, and follow through on the traditional post-interview steps and still unable to land a job. Job seekers are blamed for their inability to land a job, although it's not their fault. Below are three reasons why job seekers are not to blame:

1. **Applicant Tracking System**: Applicants are unable to know for sure if their resumes made it pass ATS screening.

2. **Data Management Technique**: Applicants are unable to anticipate which data management technique the recruiter will utilize to narrow the job pool.

3. **Uncontrollable Events in the Hiring System**: As noted in the previous chapters, there are unknown events and activities that job seekers have no control over, such as bias and discrimination and internal factors within the organization.

Because the hiring system does not fully disclose all of the steps required to land a job, it is unfair to blame job seekers for the inability to land a job.

Some critics argue the hiring system follows a logical pattern, and all of the steps in the hiring system to land a job are disclosed to job seekers. In essence, all job seekers have to do is follow the hiring system, and they will land a job.

For those people who believe job seekers are to blame for not landing a job have probably never been on the other side of the hiring system.

From the perspective of some employed people, it is difficult for them to understand the frustration, emotional turmoil and financial pressure of landing a job, although job seekers have been following the advice of HR professionals, hiring managers and career coaching experts.

5 OTHER HIDDEN REASONS

ATS, data management technique, bias and discrimination are factors which interferes with the visibility of job seekers. However, there are other hidden reasons why job seekers are having a difficult time getting the attention of recruiters and hiring managers.

- **The recruiter and hiring manager already identified a candidate they want to serve in the position before the interview phase.** It is not a secret that recruiters and hiring managers sometimes have a favorite candidate who they believe is the most qualified to serve in the role. However, they proceed to interview candidates to 'get through' the recruiting cycle just to give the appearance of fairness for compliance and liability purposes.

- **The recruiter will post an internal position to external job boards to hire an internal candidate.** Many external candidates will apply for the job only to learn the organization filled the position with an internal candidate. So, why was the internal position posted to an external job board in the first place? It is hard to say why the recruiter and hiring manager decided to post an internal job to an external job board. However, one possibility is to diversify the talent pool for Affirmative Action reporting purposes. From a compliance perspective, the recruiter and hiring manager showed they interviewed external candidates who were not qualified. So, an internal candidate was offered the job, even though hiring an internal candidate is what the recruiter and hiring manager wanted to do all along.

- **The recruiter cancels recruiting for the position due to changes to the job.** Sometimes if the recruiter and hiring manager are not happy with the qualifications of the applicant pool, they will stop the interview process to change the job description. The purpose is to attract new applicants who are more aligned with the function of the job. Applicants who previously applied will need to reapply to the position if they meet the revised qualifications in the role. Sometimes the job description changed so much from the previous one that applicants who applied to the original job find that they are no longer qualified for the revised job.

- **The recruiter and hiring manager cancel recruiting for the position altogether.** Due to internal factors, such as budgets, reorganization, mergers, and acquisitions, or a 'hiring freeze', are some of many reasons why recruiters and hiring managers discontinue recruitment for a job.

Recruiters and hiring managers are free to make changes within the hiring system as long the changes are not discriminatory. There is no telling what other factors are negatively impacting job seekers since there is no universal standard to the hiring system. Each company has its methodologies of how they assess and evaluate applicants.

As mentioned previously, the randomness of the hiring system makes it impossible for job seekers to understand the expectations of it.

6 COOLING THE THERMOMETER

The information in the previous chapters may have sparked anger about the hiring system for some job seekers. Many job seekers blame HR professionals for not telling them the truth about the hiring system. Job seekers have to navigate a hiring system which is exclusive to those who get through ATS, data management technique, bias and discrimination of recruiters and hiring managers and other uncontrollable factors.

However, some job seekers are upset with themselves for believing in a hiring system they were taught to trust by professionals. My goal in writing this book was not to upset you but to empower you, as the job seeker, with a behind-the-scenes view of the hiring system. There are so many articles written about why job seekers are not hired. As if job seekers are not hired because they are always unprepared. The blame has always been on job seekers, without recruiters and hiring managers shouldering any responsibility to how they treat job seekers in the hiring system they created. Even when job seekers ask for feedback from recruiters and hiring managers about what they can do to improve themselves, they ignore job seekers.

Recruiters and hiring managers continue to penalize job seekers for not understanding a hiring system that they created. How can job seekers improve themselves in the hiring system when recruiters and hiring manager refuse to speak with them?

What I find truly amazing is job seekers loyalty to the hiring system that has been unfair to them. The hiring system does not care if job seekers follow HR rules of hiring or not.

As I stated at the beginning of this book, the hiring system is obstructing job seekers visibility to recruiters and hiring managers.

Poorly-written resumes and less than stellar interview skills are not the reasons job seekers are unable to land a job. Forces and trends within the hiring system that are unforeseen and uncontrollable to job seekers are the sole culprits.

It is understandable that job seekers are often upset when they learn the truth about how corporate hiring works. However, rather than staying angry over it, let's channel that energy in a productive way that will help you get closer to landing a job. Besides, going rogue on HR folks will not help or improve your situation.

So, how can job seekers better position themselves within the hiring system so they can increase their visibility to recruiters and hiring managers?

7 THE BEST WAY TO GET NOTICED

Is it possible for job seekers to increase their visibility to recruiters and hiring managers when navigating the hiring system? The best and only way to get noticed is through:

1. The Advocacy of the Hiring Manager

Applicants need a sponsor to lobby their qualifications to the recruiter. The hiring manager is the only person who can tell HR which applicants he or she wants to interview. So, how does applicants get such support from the hiring manager?

What's my name?

Applicants must do some detective work by:

a. **Emailing your Resume to the Hiring Manager**
It is crucial to find the name and company email address of the hiring manager for the position[20], in addition to applying to the job on-line. Why? Because addressing the hiring manager by his or her name shows that you have initiative. Also, by personalizing your message to the hiring manager, it just looks professional.

However, finding the hiring manager's name and company email address is not easy. The work will require using social media sites such as LinkedIn to search for people within a company to find employees.

The search may also require scanning other websites such as D&B Hoovers website to perform a company search to find names of people associated with a company (Figures 3 and 4). An internet scan may reveal information where a colleague of the company attended a conference or an award ceremony.

Figure 3: D&B Hoovers Homepage

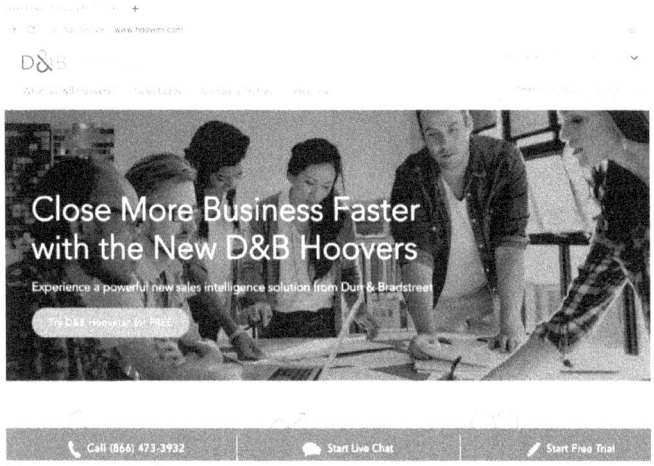

Source: www.hoovers.com

The information found on the internet may reveal clues to the name of the hiring manager or other members within the department or team.

Job seekers goal is to get their resume in front of the hiring manager, so he or she can tell HR to include your resume in the interview phase.

b. **Mailing your Resume to the Hiring Manager**

Also, mailing a hard copy of your resume[21] to the hiring manager is another option for applicants who are unable to find the hiring manager's company email address.

Figure 4: Hoovers Database

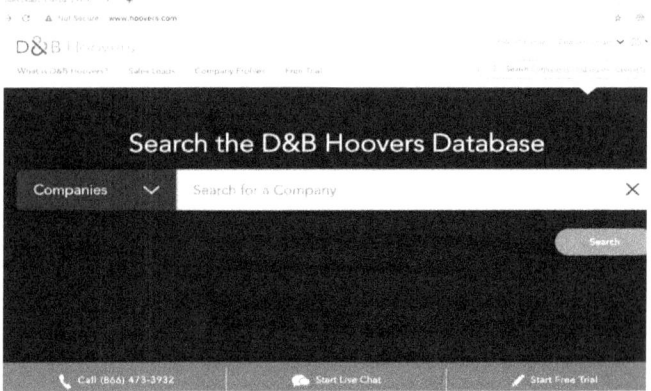

Source: www.hoovers.com

However, it is essential to note that mailing a hard copy of your resume by addressing it with a guesstimated job title will not work. The company may not have someone with an official job title of Finance Supervisor or Benefits Director.

Although those job titles do exist for some companies, that does not mean they exist within every organization. That's why it is vital to do your homework to learn 'who's who' within an organization.

The Risk

Oh, yes, there are some risks to emailing or sending a hard copy of your resume to the hiring manager.

1.   Your resume could be deleted or thrown away by the hiring manager or the assistant.
2.   The resume ends up in spam/junk folder.
3.   The hiring manager may become upset to receive your resume.

Some applicants may believe it's a good idea to call the company to receive names and email addresses of hiring managers. However, some receptionists may not disclose the names of employees nor their email addresses, although it does not hurt to try. If you have the name of the hiring manager, but not his or her company email address, then the best bet might be to mail a hard copy to the hiring manager. Again, the goal is to have the hiring manager read your resume without having ATS or HR screen it first.

Although you will not know for sure if the hiring manager will read it, at least your resume has a chance to be read by the hiring manager. With ATS it is a crapshoot if the recruiter will ever get to read it, let alone the hiring manager.

2. Employee Referral

Job seekers can increase their visibility to recruiters and hiring managers through employee referrals. Employees who have an excellent performance record and great relationships within the company are the best resources to get your resume in front of the hiring manager. The employee lobbies on your behalf about how and why you are the best person for the job. When the employee sends your resume to the hiring manager, he or she will read the resume to determine your qualifications and fit for the position. If the hiring managers agree with the employee about your skills for the job, the hiring manager will reach out to HR to add your name as a candidate for the position. Employee referrals are an excellent way to get your resume in front of the hiring manager.

3. Friends of Friends

Some applicants are surprised to learn that through friends of friends, they have an indirect connection to reach other people outside of their direct circle. Again, LinkedIn is an excellent professional website to discover connections and relationships. The hiring manager may be friends with someone you know, or your friends of friends may be associated with organizations affiliated with your hiring manager.

It is essential to find out who the hiring manager knows as well as who does your first, second, and third-level friends know. Why? So friends can introduce you to the hiring manager or people who are well connected to the hiring manager.

The purpose of sending your resume to the hiring manager is to become visible within the hiring system. Remember the executive assistant position used in the previous chapters. If over 250 applicants are applying to one position, it is vital to find an edge to get noticed. When you find individuals, who have a direct or indirect link to the hiring manager or people within his or her circle, get introduced by your first, second or third level friends to make a connection. This is no time to get skittish or docile.

4. Your Alumni

Yes, your alumni can also help you find leads to a job. On LinkedIn, the profiles show people who graduated from your school or university. This is an opportunity to introduce yourself to the LinkedIn contact as an alumnus of his or her school or university. In your message, you would inform the LinkedIn contact you have an interview at the same company and is looking for the name and email address of the hiring manager in 'X" department. The alumnus may decide to help by forwarding your resume to the hiring manager, rather than provide you his or her email address, which is fine as well. The alumnus may feel more comfortable if you state that you will keep his or her name anonymous. Again, it is a shot worth taking to get closer to an interview. If an alumnus decides not to help you, then find another alumnus who will help you get the lead. This is where the mental toughness will be needed if you are told 'no'.

An interview is not as daunting and fearful when the hiring manager and interview team knows that you were recommended for the job by someone they know and respect. Often, the halo effect can go a long way in the hiring system. In other words, if your friend is a high-performing employee, then the hiring manager, and the interview team will also assume that you will perform the same way. The good news is the hiring manager, and interview team already have a good impression about you based on your friend's stellar performance on the job.

The Status Quo of The Hiring System

You've tried the traditional route of hiring, and it's not working for you and for a lot of people who are seeking employment.

It's time to try other alternative methods to get noticed within the hiring system to land a job. Even if job seekers do not take the advice, I mentioned in this book, job seekers need to create their unique hiring system to navigate and outsmart the one HR professionals designed. It is essential to come up with your idea and ways to become visible in the hiring system. Creating your method to becoming visible to recruiters in the hiring system is much better than waiting for a recruiter who may never contact you. Job seekers must take ownership of their job search by disregarding what they have been taught about how to search and land a job.

Students Frustration in Landing a Job

Unfortunately, many schools and universities are teaching students how to find work by utilizing the traditional way of landing a job through the gates of human resources. Students do not have any idea that the system they were taught to find employment no longer works. Some career services personnel may have landed their jobs through human resources. However, they can no longer assume today's students and graduates will also land their job the same way.

Method to Landing a Job Has Changed

When my father retired from the oil refinery back in 2000, he recalled how he ended up working there. My father was a young man who served his country as a U.S. Marine during the Vietnam War. When he returned to the U.S., he needed to find work. He said that a community leader had told him the oil refinery was hiring. On the advice of the community leader, he showed up at the oil refinery, completed the job application, and interviewed on the spot by human resources. My father worked for the oil refinery for over 30 years.

I share the story about my father to make a point. The same way my father landed his job is no longer a method that I nor anyone else can duplicate. It is no longer a common practice for applicants to show up on the corporate premises to complete a paper employment application, interview with HR the same day, and know on the spot if you are hired. The process by which people land jobs has changed. There was a time when responding to an online job ad and waiting for human resources to call you was the only way to land a job. However, those days are long gone. Why? There are just too many applicants to become visible to the recruiter and hiring manager.

It is to job seekers advantage to find their way to get the attention of the recruiter to gain visibility in landing a job.

Two Reasons to 'Go Around' HR in the Hiring System?

1. Infighting between recruiters and hiring managers

There is a disconnect between recruiters and hiring managers in the quality of applicants they select and recruit to fill positions. In fact, "80 percent of recruiters believe they have a 'high' to 'very high' understanding of the jobs for which they recruit, while 61 percent of hiring managers say that recruiters have a 'low' to 'moderate' understanding of the jobs they're recruiting for"[22]. Unfortunately, there is plenty of finger-pointing between recruiters and hiring managers as to why hiring managers feel that recruiters do not understand the qualifications, they desire in candidates to fill positions. Some hiring managers blame recruiter's applicant screening process as the problem. On the other hand, recruiters blame hiring managers inability to communicate the qualifications they seek in candidates[23].

The infighting between recruiters and hiring managers supports the argument to use alternative methods to get noticed in the hiring system. The recruiter may deem an applicant unqualified, while the hiring manager may view the same resume as a qualified applicant. Applicants do not have time to wait for recruiters and hiring managers to get on the same page within the hiring system. As a result of the infighting, applicants cannot rest on the notion that recruiters and hiring managers will assess their qualifications the same way. There is a saying that sometimes people do not know what they are looking for until they see it. From the hiring manager's perspective, they may have a hard time articulating what they want in a candidate but know the qualifications when they see them.

Nevertheless, the applicant cannot allow the disconnect between recruiters and hiring managers to get in the way of landing a job.

2.   Reluctance to communicate with job seekers

Unfortunately, many applicants believe that HR will be straight with them concerning their candidacy for the position. What applicants need to keep in mind is that recruiters are managing multiple job openings with an average of 250 for each post. If a recruiter is trying to fill 20 open positions, with each post attracting about 250 applicants, the recruiter has to manage 5,000 applicants, in addition to other work responsibilities. It is unrealistic that a recruiter will want to hear from 5,000 applicants about their candidacy for a position. Trust me when I say, the recruiter does not want to hear from you. I know this is harsh, but this is the reality in the life of recruitment.

Applicants are better off calling the hiring manager, then speaking with human resources. So, if you are going to make a phone call, talk to the hiring manager[24]. There is a chance the hiring manager may speak with you concerning the status of the position. However, there is no guarantee the hiring manager will talk to you or return your call, although it is a long shot worth taking.

ACTION STEPS

❖ Apply to the on-line job <u>before</u> reaching out to the hiring manager. It is essential to officially apply to the position to be considered as an applicant.

❖ Ensure your resume is free from typos and grammatical errors as well as all correspondence to the hiring manager.

❖ Create a profile on Linkedin.com if you do not already have an account. It is essential to build and expand your professional network, in addition to finding contacts who are associated with people you want and need to know.

WHAT DO I SAY TO THE HIRING MANAGER?
(Email)

It is vital to keep your communication with the hiring manager short and positive. The goal of the email is to inform the hiring manager you applied to the position AND to provide a copy of your resume to him or her.

If the hiring manager is interested in speaking with you after reading your resume, he or she will notify HR to include your name for the interview phase (once HR confirms that you have officially applied to the position).

Your email serves as a super abbreviated cover letter without the details. Here's an email template:

Email Template to Hiring Manager

Good day, Ms. Williams,

My background is in compensation, benefits, and payroll, which might serve your needs in the role of Compensation and Rewards Analyst position. I've officially applied to the position on ABC Careers Website and wish to secure an interview with you and your team.

Below is my resume. I look forward to meeting you and your team to discuss the role!

Sincerely,

Jane Doe

When emailing the hiring manager there are two things you need to keep in mind:

1. Do not send your resume as an attachment. Instead, paste your resume in the body of the email.

2. Do not include email links.

The hiring manager may not click on your attachment nor email links in fear that they may contain a virus and decides to delete your attachment.

To be safe, remove the hyperlinks from email addresses, social media profiles, personal website, etc.

WHAT DO I SAY TO THE HIRING MANAGER?
(Hardcopy)

When mailing your resume to the hiring manager, use the same language from the email template. However, the hardcopy letter needs to be addressed to the hiring manager with his/her job title. Again, your letter serves as a super abbreviated cover letter without the details. Here's a letter template:

Letter Template to Hiring Manager

June 2, 2019
Ms. Sarah Williams, VP of Benefits and Rewards
ABC Company
123 Anyway Street
Anywhere, USA 12345

Good day, Ms. Williams,

My background is in compensation, benefits, and payroll, which might serve your needs in the role of Compensation and Rewards Analyst position I've officially applied to the position on ABC Careers Website and wish to secure an interview with you and your team.

Enclosed is my resume. I look forward to meeting you and your team to discuss the role!

Sincerely,

Jane Doe

When mailing the letter and resume to the hiring manager, please do not forget to include the hard copy of your resume.

Presentation is everything! Your letter and resume to the hiring manager appear professional when they are sent in a large manila envelope such as 9x11 or 10x13, which does not require folding the documents as with a standard 8.5 x11 envelope. The type of delivery method(United States Postal Service, UPS, FedEx, etc.,) is based on your budget.

Also, the decision to email AND mail a hard copy of your resume to the hiring manager is based on your comfort level as well. I would suggest doing both. However, if you are strapped for cash, then settle for emailing the hiring manager.

Nothing New Under the Sun

Please note that the suggestions of emailing and mailing a hard copy of your resume to the hiring manager are not new strategies. Many job seekers have not utilized the approach because the acts do not support HR's rules of hiring.

There have been plenty times in my recruiting career where a hiring manager would ask me to include an applicant's name on the interview list because the manager heard from the applicant before I even had a chance to review the applicant's resume. I've received phone calls from people who wanted to speak to the hiring manager about recommending a person for the job within the organization. Also, I've received letters of recommendations from people suggesting the hiring manager consider their friend or colleague for the position heavily. Applicants who secure advocates to help them 'sell' their skill sets and character for the job, do receive the attention of the hiring manager.

All of the strategies involved someone endorsing the skills and character of another person to serve in a job. Job seekers need an advocate on their behalf to tell HR why they need to be interviewed. This is why job seekers need to email or mail their resume to the hiring manager so he or she can serve as an advocate on their behalf to HR. Also, when applicants have people advocate for them, this tends to decrease and sometimes breakdown stereotypes and unconscious and intentional bias within the hiring system. Landing an interview is less work when someone else can speak on your behalf about your qualifications and fit for the role.

Disclaimer

Just so that I'm clear, stalking is <u>never</u> ok. Showing up at the hiring manager's place of worship or while he or she is dining out with family is inappropriate. I had an applicant who had called me on my personal cell phone. Let's just say that I was not happy. If you were not given permission to call someone's personal number, then do not do it! Also, harassing people is not cool either. Stalking and harassing people will land you in jail – which is not the result we are looking for. Professional folks do not do the above mentioned acts, so use your professional judgment.

8 HR's REBUTTAL

Many traditional human resources professionals will challenge the advice I provided in this book. They will tell job seekers the alternative methods outlined in this book to land a job are unfounded and erroneous. As noted in Chapter 1, they will insist that you continue to follow their status quo of the hiring system by believing:

- The hiring system is fair.
- The hiring system will showcase job seekers qualifications.
- The hiring cycle produces the best of the best candidate for the position.
- The hiring system is logical.
- Job seekers who were not hired did not follow all of the HR rules and hire experts advice.
- Recruiters want to get to know the real you in the hiring system.
- The only method to land a job is through the traditional steps and iron gates of HR.

Traditional recruiters believe it is job seekers fault for being out of work for an extended period because they do not know how to navigate the hiring system. As I mentioned earlier, job seekers have tried to land a job through the rules and steps HR professionals have created. The hiring system has worked well for them because they have control over every aspect of it. To control the hiring system, human resources professionals will tell job seekers to refrain from calling them. As I mentioned earlier, recruiters and HR professionals are not interested in speaking with job seekers about their candidacy for the job. Recruiters are concerned they will say something the job seekers may interpret as discriminatory. Recruiters have control over how much or little information they communicate with job seekers.

Job seekers have not benefited under the hiring system because every company's selection and hiring method is different. Also, HR professionals and hiring managers do not disclose all of the methods they use to evaluate job seeker's fitness for the job. The randomness of the hiring system is impossible for job seekers to gain a competitive edge because there is no universal standard for hiring.

Remember, there is more than one way to land a job, contrary to HR's rules of hiring!

9 PRELUDES TO LETTER TO JAKE

Recruiter's Transition to a Future-Focused Method of Hiring from 2030 and Beyond, discussed the future of hiring which featured a letter an applicant sent to a recruiter named Jake. The letter explained the hiring system from the applicant's perspective while asking Jake to make changes to the method in which his company selects and hires people.

Although the letter is fictious, the purpose of it serves to capture the frustration, contradictory, and hypocrisy job seekers experience when trying to land a job in the hiring system. Millions of job seekers who go through the hiring system complain about the lack of personable interaction and response from recruiters. Also, if job seekers desire to work, they should be able to do so without deception, bias, and exploitation. Many job seekers experience the same 24 issues which are bolded in the applicant's letter.

I decided to include the letter in this book to reiterate the point about the randomness of the hiring system and the inability of job seekers to change it. The only hope for job seekers is to leverage the hiring system by creating their own 'systems' to gain an advantage in landing a job.

The *Letter to Jake* serves as a reminder that waiting on HR to call after applying to a position is simply a waste of your time and resources.

10 A LETTER TO JAKE

Dear Mr. Jake,

I'm a competent and fabulous online candidate who wants to work for your remarkable organization. I possess the required knowledge, skills and abilities to the advertised position to meet your company goals. However, I am not too fond of your hiring process because when I go online to research your company on social media to talk to a recruiter about your company and to join any community engagement forums to exchange information, there is **little or no social media presence from your company**.

Before I apply to a job from your company, I would like to see active communication from a recruiter on Facebook, LinkedIn or even on your company website. What are you doing to engage me as a potential candidate? I would love to network with you while reviewing job openings, receiving job alerts about open positions and even submitting an online application from my smartphone, but I can't because your **hiring process is not mobile friendly**. I would love to do all of this on my smartphone. Your website claims that you all seek tech-savvy, innovative candidates, but your hiring process is not mobile friendly. What is wrong with this picture? Your company has quite a few positions that I'm interested in applying; however, your **job descriptions are so outdated**.

Does your company really want candidates to know how to use a pager, a PDA Palm Pilot, word processor, and a dictaphone in the 21st century? Why are you not reviewing job descriptions to ensure they reflect current skillsets? Are you lazy or believe candidates will not notice or care? Of course, it is so convenient that I can't even let you know that your job descriptions are outdated because you **never include your contact information on the job ad**.

Also, your **job ads are employer-centered**. The job ads always list what the company wants and demand from candidates. Do you even care about my needs as a candidate? Well, you should if you want me to work for your company. By the way, do you expect me to spend 45-60 minutes to complete an online job application? That is way too long. At least explain to me why your **online job application is so lengthy** to help me understand your process. What burns me up about your hiring process is that you ask me to fill out the online application, upload my resume, cover letter and other information about me, although you never read them. Why is it that you **never read my resume or cover letter** when you ask me for this information? Do you enjoy wasting my time? If you do not plan to read them, then stop asking me to include the documentation in the hiring process.

It is essential to my family that I find work so I can support them. I know you can relate since you have a family to support as well. Wouldn't it be nice to see the salary and compensation package for the job so that I can make an informed decision? I do not understand why you **keep the salary and compensation package hidden** from me. Is my livelihood a game to you? If I knew the compensation package, then I can determine whether I want to apply to the job, so I don't waste your time, and you do not waste mine. Besides, wouldn't it suck that I turn down the position at the end of the hiring process because the salary was too low? If you let me know the salary

upfront, we can avoid this. On the other hand,

maybe you enjoy **withholding information**

which would help me make an informed

decision about working for you.

Although I spent over an hour completing the

online job application, submitting the required

documentation and the optional self-identify

forms, **I never hear back from you**. Why? I

find it rude and unprofessional that you never

informed me of my candidate status for the

position. Your silence is equivalent to me

taking you out to dinner, paying the bill, and

ignoring my phone call to you the next day and the next. Are the leadership and staff rude at your company as well? Since you choose to ignore me as a candidate, I will return the favor by telling my friends, family, and colleagues about my experience with your company and refrain from buying your products and services, since you have a nasty communication problem.

Maybe the reason you ignore me as a candidate because you are **clueless about the people you want to hire**. Do you ignore me because I don't fit in? If so, then please have the courage and professionalism to tell me so I can move on to another employer who is clear about the type of people they want to hire. By the way, are there **no 'humans' in the human resources department**? Why in the world am I **receiving emails from robots**? Your communication with me is so impersonal and cold. Would it kill you to address me by my name instead of "Dear Candidate"? When I send you my cover letter, you penalized me for using "Dear Recruiter" and tell your colleagues that I didn't do my homework to learn your name or the hiring manager's name.

Well, as a recruiter, you need to address me by my name on documentation during the hiring process. You already have my name and contact information, so what's the problem? When I finally get to meet you on the phone for the first time, I was so thrilled and excited to meet you. However, **my interaction with you was less than stellar**. You, as the Recruiter was my first impression with your company, and it was awful. As the Recruiter, you were just flat, unengaging and lacked excitement about talking to me about your company. When you were talking to me, you stuck to a script and had no intentions to get to know me as a person who could be a part of your organization. I guess your inability to engage with me explains why you were so **inflexible when it came to the interview schedule**.

I still can't believe you made me interview with you the day after my father's funeral and threaten to drop me as a candidate if I didn't stick to your interview schedule. Then you continued to ask me brainteaser and stupid interview questions which had no relevance to my qualifications to perform in the job. I have no idea what animal would describe my personality. I'm tired of

rehearsing the same old interview

questions. Such as, where do you see yourself

in five years? What are your strengths and

weaknesses? Describe a time when you felt

pressured to perform? These questions are

such as waste of your time and mine as if you

can tell if I'm qualified for the job based on my

responses. Give me a break. My favorite

question is, "Tell me about yourself?" If you

had read my resume, cover letter, personal

website, and Linked-in profile, you would

already know about my background and other

accomplishments, qualifications, professional and personal goals. Do your homework.

Your interview questions **do not provide or expose candidates to the nature of your company culture.** When was the last time you reviewed your interview questions? After I practiced rehearsing the same old tired behavioral interview questions as part of the hiring process, you hired an internal candidate. My question to you is why did you **post an open position to an external job board just to hire an internal candidate**? Once again, you have wasted my time. I had to take off work, lie to my current employer to why I needed the day off, just to show up for the face-to-face interview so that you can hire an internal candidate? Really? So, you call this process fair?

The **current hiring process is very biased and discriminatory**. After you met me face-to-face, for some reason, I'm no longer qualified for the job. I answered every behavioral interview question fully and truthfully with examples of how I solve problems and can add value to your team and organization. I articulated my accomplishments and results to you. My qualifications have not changed from the phone screen. I have demonstrated to you I have the experience and intellectual acumen to contribute and deliver results to your organization fairly quickly. But for some reason, I'm not good enough to serve in the role now.

Did I make you or the hiring manager uncomfortable with my authentic self? Was my confidence misconstrued as arrogance? Did my gender, race, accent, color, and overall appearance offend you and the hiring manager? Am I not someone who could represent your company? Well, I will not apologize for being who I am and what I am. Your perceptions and biases of who should serve in a role will lead your company to lose valuable and diverse people who can produce results for your organization. Maybe you **don't care about the candidate online hiring experience, and neither does the hiring manager.** If this is not the case, then why do you continue to support an impersonal hiring process to find and select candidates? I find it ironic that you **want to hire 'perfect' candidates for the job**, but people are not 'perfect.' The candidate in your head that you believe is the perfect one does not exist.

Although you say that you **only want to hire Ivy league candidates** to fill the position, again, you miss out on people who can perform in the job other than Ivy league candidates.

Besides, why would you assume that only Ivy league candidates can do the job? Where did you get that assumption? The **hiring process is so long** and drags for months because you are trying to find the perfect candidate that you concocted in your head. Maybe another reason your hiring process is so long because your **organization is slow to make decisions**. I understand that you want to be sure the candidate can perform the job; however, does it take months to figure it out?

Do you expect me as the candidate to wait it out for months until you make up your mind? I submitted my online job application, resume, cover letter, education credentials, accomplishments, and participated in the face-to-face interview, in addition to information on my social media profiles – and you still can't determine if I'm the right person for the job? You should know within 2-3 days after our face-to-face meeting if you want to hire me, not months.

This is why your candidates are unhappy with your hiring process. I want to work for your company, but you have issues and concerns about your hiring process which needs to be addressed. Please consider making changes to your hiring process to stay relevant.

Sincerely,
Your potential candidate, job candidate and future employee

11 GOOD AND BAD DAYS

There are two things you must do in the midst of your job search:

1. Keep Your Sanity

Without your sanity, the ability to focus and keep your mind and spirit in a positive formation will become a challenge. Why should you stay in positive spirits? Well, the worst thing that can happen to you as a job seeker is to land an interview with an employer and the pressures and frustrations of the job search seeps into your interview. How? Through the negative vibes or aura of job seekers. The draining presence can sabotage their chances of landing a job because no one wants to hire people who are perceived to be negative.

Unfortunately, recruiters and hiring managers do not extend grace or empathy within the hiring system. Recruiters and hiring managers will assume your negative nature is who you are as a person and not because of your circumstances of being out of work for so long. Sometimes, the pressures and frustration of the job search are evident based on job seekers attitudes, choice of words, and how they articulate the outlook of their situation. Sometimes bad situations even make habitually positive people not become their best selves.

As I said earlier, the employer does not care or take into consideration the toll of the job search has on people looking for work. It is equivalent to telling a hungry person to act as if he is not hungry and punishing him for showing the signs of needing and wanting to eat. The notion of masking or ignoring the frustrations of the job search in an interview situation is difficult. Some people find it inhuman to suppress the evidence of job search burnout, because we are all human beings with basic needs which must be met for all of us to stay in positive spirits.

So, how do you keep your sanity?

People who are masters at maintaining a positive and optimistic spirit knows how to control the negative energy that emerges within them from time to time. There will be bad days which the negative energy will try to take over your day or even your life. To keep your sanity in check, job seekers must have a plan to get rid of negative energy, so it does not stay with them. People who maintain a positive spirit have a plan, ritual, or something that they do to purge the negative thoughts and energy from their minds and bodies.

When I'm in a bad mood, I get on my elliptical trainer and power peddle for 15 minutes. The power peddling helps me get rid of any 'mad' or nervous energy to keep my mind sane and focused. Some people may walk, write down their thoughts, meditate, or other activities to maintain a healthy, positive mind.

When the negative energy emerges, what do you do with it? Do you let it take control of your thoughts and actions? Job seekers must come up with their own way to get rid of the negative energy, so it does not settle and rest on them. The negative energy has to go somewhere, so how do you release yours? It is essential to have an outlet for negative energy. Why?

Let's say, you received three automated rejection emails in one week. Yes, you will feel disappointed, frustrated, and even angry when life does not meet your needs and expectations. So, do you beat yourself up over the disappointment? Do you carry that resentment or frustration to the coffee shop, the supermarket or home to your family? It is vital to your mental health to create some ritual to help you stay positive during the job search.

Job Search Depression

Another reason to maintain a positive and optimistic outlook is job search depression. Many job seekers experience job search depression when they are unable to land a job within 8 to 12 weeks of looking for work[25]. The feeling of frustration, despair, and hopelessness is normal. However, these feelings can also get in the way of landing a job. So, the importance of staying on top of your mental health is critical.

There are many articles which talk about job search depression and what can be done to offset or minimize the negative emotions. I will include some of the articles in the back of this book. There may be untapped ideas and methods in the articles to help strengthen your mind and soul. Again, if you google 'job search depression,' you find plenty of articles.

2. Add Skillsets to Your Resume

While you are job searching, it is important to maintain or learn new skills[26]. At some point, an employer will want to know how you managed your time while job searching.

Volunteer

Volunteer some of your time to a company, organization or association to maintain a skillset or learn a new one. The opportunity could lead to meeting people who can help you land a job or introduce you to contacts which can lead to employment.

Free On-line Courses

Some organizations such as the Foundation Center[1] and Udemy.com offer free on-line courses to maintain a skillset or learn a new one. To find additional free on-line courses, just type 'free on-line courses' in the Google search engine to discover what's available.

---

[1] https://foundationcenter.org/

Write Blogs and Articles

A great way to solidify your expertise is to write blogs and articles about what you know or have a deep passion about. There are free websites and blog sites where you can begin to create your on-line platform. Although with free websites, you may need to optimize your website to make it visible in a search engine such as Google.

Be Creative and Stay Busy

Job seekers need to become creative in finding ways to add skills to their resumes. There is more than one way to learn new skills to stay relevant. Also, it just helps to keep busy during a job search to take your mind off the monotony of looking for work. It is essential to create a routine to decrease your chances of becoming bored and depressed. I always find it helpful to exercise every day, whether it's taking a walk around the neighborhood, peddling on the elliptical bike or working out with a video trainer. Even going to a coffee shop or library to read will help break the monotony of the job search. As long as the routine works to keep you in a positive state of mind, then, stick with it.

12 THE ENDLESS DOGFIGHT

Your family needs you. The fight to preserve or improve your family's lifestyle begins with you. As I mentioned in the previous chapters, landing a job will require mental toughness and endurance, which must sustain you throughout the dogfight. Yes, I'm using the analogy of a dogfight to land a job. Why? If you ever watched two dogs fight or even animal documentaries where they show animals such as bears, elephants, and lions fighting, notice how they do not back down from a challenge. When other animals threaten their territory, they are willing to fight to the death to protect and preserve their family. As a job seeker, you must possess the mental toughness to fight for your right to have a quality of life by landing a job.

Many people follow the rules because that's what law-abiding citizens are called to do. However, what if HR's rules to landing a job were holding you back from a quality of life? What if the rules for landing a job were no longer working for you? If you have been out of work for six months, one year, two years or longer, do you continue to follow HR's rules to landing a job? Sometimes, while you are in the dogfight, you will need to surprise your enemy with a new strategy to catch them off guard to get what you need to survive. Although I shared some ways to leverage the hiring system, ultimately, job seekers must create their own 'system' to land a job. The enemy, in this case, is the hiring system and those who support the status quo of hiring. I know some people may not equate finding a job to a dogfight, but that is precisely the situation. How? Job seekers are fighting biases, discrimination, ATS, data management technique, and company's internal practices. In addition to all other forces and trends which are unknown and uncontrollable in landing a job.

Also, your approach to the method in which you are looking for employment must change to create an intervention. So, creating an intervention starts with a renewed mindset of what the hiring system is and is not. Once the reality of the hiring system is accepted, is where you, as the job seeker, can begin to strategize a new way to become a visible applicant and candidate within the hiring system.

The Future of Work

Until recruiters change the method in which they select and hire people, job seekers will need to rely on their creativity and initiative to landing a job. Job seekers who sit back and wait for HR to call them rather than create their own opportunities will continue to lack the resources they need to survive.

In the 21st century and beyond, job seekers will need to create their opportunities to make things happen for themselves. Today is the last day the traditional way of landing a job will hold you back.

You Can Do This!

As a job seeker, you have the ability and tenacity to land a job. However, it requires being bold, relentless, creative, and unafraid to step outside your comfort zone. As well as ignoring what other people will think or say about you. Also, landing a job will require hearing 'no' a lot, but you already know that. Just remember, if you stop looking for work, you will never receive a 'yes, we would like to extend a job offer to you.'

Yes, you will land a job!

SOME UNCONVENTIONAL WAYS PEOPLE LANDED JOBS

Below are some ways people have landed jobs. I included a few sources at the end of this chapter. Although these methods have worked for some people, they may not work for others. Again, it is vital to create your own system to land a job.

- Name dropping

- Sending a cover letter with a sense of humor

- Placing your resume on a billboard

- Creating YouTube Videos to sell your skillsets

- Handing out your resumes as flyers

- Creating Facebook and Google Ads

- Posting your qualifications on Pinterest

- Turning your resume into a Google Map

- Wearing your resume on a T-shirt

- Starting a passion project

- Placing your resume on business cards

- Creating a LinkedIn Slideshare PowerPoint to showcase qualifications

The common theme in these unconventional methods is the ability and courage for job seekers to step outside of their comfort zone.

As mentioned previously in this book, going through human resources is not the only avenue which leads to employment. There are job seekers who are landing jobs through less traditional routes.

Sources

Ayodeji Onibalusi. "The most unconventional ways people landed their dream jobs." *Glassdoor.com.* (March 19, 2019). Retrieved on August 4, 2019 from https://www.glassdoor.com/blog/the-most-unconventional-ways-people-landed-their-dream-jobs/

Danielle Braff. "10 brilliantly creative ways people have gotten jobs." *Mentalfloss.com.* (June 8, 2017). Retrieved on August 4, 2019 from http://mentalfloss.com/article/501588/10-brilliantly-creative-ways-people-have-gotten-jobs

J.T O'Donnell. **"If You Want a New Job in 2018, This 1 (Unconventional) Step Could Speed Things Up**." *Inc.com*. (December 19, 2017). Retrieved on August 4, 2019 from https://www.inc.com/jt-odonnell/if-you-want-a-new-job-in-2018-this-1-unconventional-step-could-speed-things-up.html

Sheiresa Ngo. "The Most Ridiculous Ways People Apply for a Job in Today's Economy." *Cheatsheet.com*. (February 13, 2018). Retrieved on August 4, 2019 from https://www.cheatsheet.com/money-career/looking-for-a-job-crazy-ways-to-get-hired.html/

Brianna Steinhilber. "5 unconventional ways to find your dream job and get hired." *Nbcnews.com*. (september 19, 2018). Retrieved on August 4, 2019 from https://www.nbcnews.com/better/business/5-unconventional-ways-find-your-dream-job-get-hired-ncna910396

Jacqulyn Smith. "20 creative things job seekers have done to get noticed." Forbes.com. (August 13, 2013). Retrieved on August 4, 2019 from **https://www.forbes.com/sites/jacquelynsmith/2013/08/15/20-creative-things-job-seekers-have-done-to-get-noticed/#134293e034b9**

Stephanie Walden. "Out-of-the-Box Approaches to the Job Search (That Actually Work)." *Mashable.com.* (July 19, 2014). Retrieved on August 4, 2019 from https://mashable.com/video/tech-apologies/

THE BEST REASON WHY YOU ARE FABULOUS

You are unique:

★ No one in the world thinks like you.

★ No one in the world has the outlook and skillsets that you possess.

★ The knowledge and experience you bring to any relationship add value to others whether they know it or not.

★ You do not allow temporary situations to dictate your future.

★ You are not afraid to test the unknown because you are a fighter.

★ You do not allow negative words and

ideas to live and permeate your soul.

★ Your ability to stay focus gives you strength.

★ Your mental toughness is second to none.

★ You are unique because you are an answer to someone's problem.

★ There is unfinished business that you and only you can complete while you are still living and breathing.

ABOUT THE AUTHOR

Dr. Chalette Renee Griffin graduated from Regent University School of Business and Leadership from Virginia Beach, VA with a Doctorate in Strategic Leadership with a concentration in Strategic Foresight. She served as an Adjunct Instructor at Wave Leadership College in Virginia Beach where she taught undergraduate and adult students leadership principles from a biblical and secular perspective.

Dr. Griffin has been selected as a peer reviewer for the *Journal of Human Resources Management and is a SHRM certified HR professional (SHRM-CP) from the Society for Human Resource Management (SHRM).*

She recently published her book on **Amazon.com** titled, *Recruiter's transition to a future-focused method of hiring from 2030 and beyond,* where she makes an intellectual case why recruiters need to change the way they select and hire people.

Please visit Dr. Griffin's website at
www.foresight-for-the-new-age-recruiter.com

METHODS TO COMBAT JOB SEARCH DEPRESSION

Mark Anthony Dyson. 'Five ways to fight job search depression today and tomorrow." *Thevoiceofjob seekers.com*. Retrieved on August 2, 2019 from https://thevoiceofjob seekers.com/job-search-depression/

Alyssa Fusek. "Why Job Hunting Sucks When You Have Anxiety and Depression." Themighty.com.(April 29, 2018). Retrieved on August 2, 2019 from https://themighty.com/2018/04/unemployed-looking-for-a-job-anxiety-depression/

Micaela Marini Higgs. "How to deal with job search depression." Nytimes.com. (May 27, 2019).Retrieved on August 2, 2019. https://www.nytimes.com/2019/05/27/smarter-living/how-to-deal-with-job-search-depression.html

Gloria Kopp. "7 Causes of Job search Depression and How to Prevent It." *Careerpivot.com*. Retrieved on August 2, 2019 from https://careerpivot.com/2017/7-causes-job-search-depression-prevent/

Greg Kratz. "What to do if your job search is making you depressed." *Flexjobs.com* (January 8, 2019). Retrieved on August 2, 2019 from https://www.flexjobs.com/blog/post/what-to-do-if-job-search-making-you-depressed/

Jennifer Liberto. "The Unemployed Psyche: Job Searching for Long Crushed My Soul." *Money.Cnn.com*.(August 8, 2014) https://money.cnn.com/2014/08/05/news/economy/longterm-unemployed-depression/index

J.T. O'Donnell. "The Psychological Impact of Job Search in 2019." *Inc.com*. (February 18, 2019). Retrieved on August 2, 2019 from https://www.inc.com/jt-odonnell/the-psychological-impact-of-job-search-in-2019.html

Joan E. Mullinax, M.Ed., LPC. "Dealing with Anxiety & Depression in the Job Search." *EddinsCounseling.com*. (August 4, 2014). Retrieved on August 2, 2019 from https://eddinscounseling.com/dealing-anxiety-depression-job-search/

Sarah Rodrigues, Ph.D. "5 Tips To Help PhDs Overcome Frustration And Depression While Job Hunting." *Cheekyscientist.com*. Retrieved on August 2, 2019 from https://cheekyscientist.com/5-tips-to-help-phds-overcome-frustration-depression-while-job-hunting/

ENDNOTES

[1] U.S. Department of Labor Office. "Internet Applicant Record Keeping Rules". *Office of Federal Contract Compliance Programs.* Retrieved on June 9, 2019. https://www.dol.gov/ofccp/regs/compliance/faqs/iappfaqs.htm#Q2GI

[2] Jim Womack. "Purpose, Process, People". *Lean Enterprise Institute* (June 12, 2006). Retrieved on June 12, 2019. https://www.lean.org/womack/DisplayObject.cfm?o=742

[3] D.L. Kauffman Jr., Systems one: An introduction to systems thinking. (St. Paul, MN: Future Systems / TLH Associates, 1980), 1

[4] Virginia Anderson & Lauren Johnson. Systems thinking basics: from concepts to casual loops. (Acton, Massachusetts: Leverage Networks, Inc. 1997), 2

[5] Alison Doyle. "How to get your resume past the applicant tracking system." *The Balance Careers.com.* (May 17, 2019). Retrieved on June 1, 2019. https://www.thebalancecareers.com/how-to-get-your-resume-past-the-applicant-tracking-system-2063135

[6] Glasssdoor Team. "50 Recruiting Stats That Will Make You Think". *Glassdor For Employers.* (January 20, 2015). Retrieved on June 27, 2019. https://www.glassdoor.com/employers/blog/50-hr-recruiting-stats-make-think/

[7] Peter Economy. "11 Interesting Hiring Statistics You Should Know." *Inc.com.* (May 5, 2015). Retrieved on June 13, 2019. https://www.inc.com/peter-economy/19-interesting-hiring-statistics-you-should-know.html

[8] Chalette Renee Griffin. "Recruiter's transition to a future-focused method of hiring from 2030 and beyond." (Amazon.com) June 3, 2019.

[9] Chalette Renee Griffin, "Recruiter's transition to a future-focused method of hiring from 2030 and beyond."

[10] Business Linkedin.com. "The Ultimate List of Hiring Statistics for Hiring Manager, HR Professionals and Recruiters". *Linkedin Talent Solutions.* Retrieved on June 20, 2019. https://business.linkedin.com/content/dam/business/talent-solutions/global/en_us/c/pdfs/Ultimate-List-of-Hiring-Stats-v02.04.pdf

[11] "What is Affirmative Action and Why Was It Created?" *Hg.org Legal Resources.* Retrieved on June 7, 2019. https://www.hg.org/legal-articles/what-is-affirmative-action-and-why-was-it-created-31524

[12] U.S. Department of Labor. "Affirmative Action". Retrieved on June 1, 2019. https://www.dol.gov/general/topic/hiring/affirmativeact

[13] State of Wisconsin Bureau of Procurement. "Affirmative Action Goals". *Vendornet System*. Retrieved on June 5, 2019. http://vendornet.state.wi.us/vendornet/contract/goals.asp

[14] Alexandre Tanzi and Shelly Hagan. "Half of Americans Are Now Over the Age of 38." *Bloomberg.com* (June 20, 2019). Retrieved on June 27, 2019.
 https://www.bloomberg.com/news/articles/2019-06-20/half-of-americans-are-now-over-the-age-of-38-census-data-show

[15] Allison Doyle. "What is an applicant tracking system?" *Thebalancecareers.com*. (January 29, 2019). Retrieved on July 12, 2019. https://www.thebalancecareers.com/what-is-an-applicant-tracking-systems-ats-2061926

[16] Allison Doyle, "What is an applicant tracking system?"

[17] Matt Deutsch. "What is ATS, and how does it work?" *TopEchelon.com*. (June 14, 2019). Retrieved on July 12, 2019 from https://www.topechelon.com/blog/owner-issues/what-exactly-is-an-applicant-tracking-system/

[18] U.S. Department of Labor Office. "Internet Applicant Record Keeping Rules"

[19] U.S. Department of Labor Office. "Internet Applicant Record Keeping Rules"

[20] Marc Cenedella "Tricking the system into giving you interviews". Ladders.com.(July 29, 2019). Retrieved on July 29, 2019. https://www.theladders.com/career-advice/tricking-the-system-into-giving-you-interviews

[21] Marc Cendella, "Tricking the system into giving you interviews."

[22] Nathan Brumby. "61% of Hiring Managers Report A Failure on The Part of Recruiters". *MightyRecruiter.com* (January 11, 2017). Retrieved on June 17, 2019. https://www.mightyrecruiter.com/blog/61-of-hiring-managers-report-a-failure-on-the-part-of-recruiters/

[23] Forbes Human Resources Council. "13 Most Common Hiring Process Bottlenecks and How to Correct Them." *Forbes.com* (July 11, 2017). Retrieved on June 6, 2019. https://www.forbes.com/sites/forbeshumanresourcescounc il/2017/07/11/13-most-common-hiring-process-bottlenecks-and-how-to-correct-them/#60896fca74d0

[24] Joe Turner. "A Follow-up Call Wins the Interview."

[25] Micaela Marini Higgs. How to deal with job search depression. Nytimes.com. (May 27, 2019).Retrieved on August 2, 2019. https://www.nytimes.com/2019/05/27/smarter-living/how-to-deal-with-job-search-depression.html

[26] Micaela Marini Higgs. "How to deal with job search depression."

LIST OF FIGURES AND TABLES

Figures

Tables

INDEX

A

Advantage	7, 16, 54, 64
Advocate	61
Affirmative Action Plan	25, 26, 32, 41
Alternative	7, 9, 52, 55, 62
Alumni	51
Applicant Pool	32, 34, 37, 38, 42
Applicant Tracking System	11, 13, 16, 31, 33, 35, 39
Assumptions	7, 20, 23
Application	6, 16, 24, 25, 28,30,31,53,54, 66,68,69,71, 82
Automated Rejection Letters	11, 31, 35, 37, 86

B

Behavioral Interview Questions	22, 39, 77,78

Create an Intervention	6, 90
Create Own System	89
Creative	88, 91
Criteria	15,25, 32, 33, 34, 35, 36ht, 37

D

Database	31, 32, 48
Depression	10, 86, 87
Discrimination	9, 25, 28, 29, 30, 39, 41, 44, 90
Dogfight	10, 89, 90

E

Employee Referral	50
Employment	6, 9, 11, 12, 24, 26, 28, 31, 52, 54, 87, 90, 93
Equal Employment Opportunity	26, 28
Expectations	8, 11, 20, 43, 86
Experts	14, 20, 21, 22, 40, 62

F

G

H

I

J

O

P

Q

R

S

Satisfy	26
Search	9, 10, 11, 18, 27, 32, 37, 47, 53, 65, 84,85,86,87,88
Skillsets	20, 67, 87,92, 96
Solely	8, 9, 18
Status Quo	9, 52, 62, 90
Step	7, 17, 13, 14, 15, 21, 37, 39, 40, 56, 62, 91, 93
Strategy	18, 23, 89
Successfully	12, 22
System	6-12-23, 26 28-33, 35, 37,38, 39, 40, 42, 43, 44,45, 46, 51-55,61, 62, 63, 64, 89, 90, 92

T

Technical	12, 16, 27
Tell	12, 14, 25, 42, 44, 46, 48, 61, 62, 72, 73, 76, 84
Terms	6, 27
Time	7, 11, 12, 15, 18, 20, 21, 26, 36, 39, 41, 51, 52, 54, 55, 60, 61, 64, 69, 70, 74, 76, 77, 85, 87, 88
Trends	16, 45, 90
Trust	20, 44, 56
Try	27, 29, 49, 52, 55, 56, 81, 85

U

Undependable	16
Unemployed	12, 14, 24
Unidentified	15
Universal	16, 43, 63
Unsuccessful	9

www.ingramcontent.com/pod-product-compliance
Lightning Source LLC
Chambersburg PA
CBHW072214170526
45158CB00002BA/589